Granny Square Style

How to Make Limitless Projects
from 10 Classic Patterns

BELTS · PILLOWS
AFGHANS · SCARVES
TOTES

HYLLAM LEFÈVRE

SCHIFFER
CRAFT
4880 Lower Valley Road • Atglen, PA 19310

Welcome

I'm Hyllam Lefèvre, also known as Le Crochet de Plume. I learned needlework at an early age, and initially studied to be a lawyer. One thing led to another, and with the encouragement of my husband and my wonderful little boy, I embarked on a new adventure: crocheting.

Crocheting is much more than a passion for me. It provides meditation and motivation, and it's a powerful outlet! When I create designs, I like to draw inspiration from my surroundings, from discussions with my community, and from my state of mind.

What inspires me as much as creating is meeting and developing real friendships with people: meeting up over a coffee, exchanging messages online, and so on. Please join me on Le Crochet de Plume on social media (YouTube, Instagram, Pinterest, Facebook) or visit my website, www.lecrochetdeplume.com. **The QR codes offer you how-to videos** on my YouTube channel. Even though I'm speaking in my native language, there are English subtitles, and these videos explain every skill visually for you. See you soon!

Other Schiffer Craft Books on Related Subjects:

PixlPeople: Cross-Stitch Your Favorite People, John-Michael Stoof, ISBN 978-0-7643-6191-3

Summer Knitting for Little Sweethearts: 40 Nordic-Style Warm Weather Patterns for Girls, Boys, and Babies, Hanne Andreassen Hjelmås and Torunn Steinsland, ISBN 978-0-7643-6606-2

The Little Guide to Mastering Your Sewing Machine: All the Sewing Basics, Plus 15 Step-by-Step Projects, Sylvie Blondeau, ISBN 978-0-7643-4970-6

English-language edition copyright ©2025 by Schiffer Publishing, Ltd.

Originally published as *Granny Squares Faciles*, ©2023 by Éditions Eyrolles, Paris. Translated from the French by Ordentop Agency.

Library of Congress Control Number: 2024942484

Designed by Aurore Élie, Éditions Eyrolles
Illustrations, pages 4, 20, 66: Shutterstock/OKing
Instruction photographs and page 7: Hyllam Lefèvre
Drawings and diagrams: Anne-Sophie Ryo
Styled photographs: Fabrice Besse

Type set in Megan Display and Acumin

ISBN: 978-0-7643-6895-0

Printed in India

Published by Schiffer Craft
An imprint of Schiffer Publishing, Ltd.
4880 Lower Valley Road
Atglen, PA 19310
Phone: (610) 593-1777; Fax: (610) 593-2002
Email: Info@schifferbooks.com
Web: www.schifferbooks.com

For our complete selection of fine books on this and related subjects, please visit our website at www.schifferbooks.com. You may also write for a free catalog.

Schiffer Publishing's titles are available at special discounts for bulk purchases for sales promotions or premiums. Special editions, including personalized covers, corporate imprints, and excerpts, can be created in large quantities for special needs. For more information, contact the publisher.

We are always looking for people to write books on new and related subjects. If you have an idea for a book, please contact us at proposals@schifferbooks.com.

Contents

PART 1

Crochet Materials and Techniques

Materials

Being comfortable and having fun are essential aspects of crocheting.
A simple crochet hook and basic yarn are all you need to get started. But the more you get hooked (!), the more you'll want to acquire the materials that inspire you.

Hooks

When you choose your hook, pay attention to its

- *material:* aluminum, wood, bamboo, stainless steel, or plastic;
- *handle:* cylindrical or with a flattened area for better grip; and
- *diameter:* hooks can range from 0.6 mm on the small end to 20 mm and up for the largest.

The choice of crochet hook is a personal one and will depend on your experience and your individual grip.

The choice of hook size, on the other hand, is determined by the type of project and the size of yarn used. The recommended hook sizes for the granny squares in this book are listed with each square's instructions in Part 2.

Yarns

The look of your final work will depend on your yarn.

There are many different fibers available (acrylic, cotton, wool, linen, merino, and more), with different thicknesses (fine, medium, and thick) and textures ranging from soft to stiff, as well as mercerized yarns. So it's important to choose the right yarn for your project.

Yarn should be matched to the type of project you're working on. Usually, it's fine yarns for baby clothes, medium yarns for other garments, and thick yarns for accessories or home textiles.

Just as with the squares in Part 2, the recommended yarn size and hook size for each project in Part 3 are specified in the instructions. By referring to the label on the yarn, you can find its info and then choose the yarn best suited to your project, and often the label includes care tips to ensure your creation stands the test of time.

For beginners, making granny squares is the ideal way to discover a wide variety of yarns, both in terms of color and texture. So, take the time to select the yarns and colors that inspire you for your projects.

For this book's projects and photographs, I used yarns from the Lou Passion brand, one that makes for beautiful combinations and results.

- Aquarelle (50 g ball, 125 m): 100% natural cotton certified OEKO-TEX standard 100. Hook size: 2.5 mm to 3.5 mm.
- Emmy (50 g ball, 85 m): 100% cotton yarn. Hook size: 3.5 mm to 4 mm.
- Elana (50 g ball, 140 m): 100% acrylic yarn. Hook size: 3.5 mm to 4 mm.
- Tricoton (250 g ball, 225 m): 85% cotton/25% polyester yarn. Hook size: 4 mm to 5 mm.
- Naya (100 g ball, 65 m): 100% acrylic yarn. Hook size: 6 mm to 8 mm.

In Parts 2 and 3, you'll also find details of the yarns used.

Supplies

In addition to the basic materials above, you'll need a few extra supplies:

- Stitch markers: useful for indicating the start of rounds and keeping track of stitch counts.
- Scissors for cutting yarn.
- Tapestry needles with a large enough eye to easily insert yarns at the finishing stage.

- A tape measure, essential for custom creations and for blocking squares, to ensure they are the correct size.
- Pins and a foam mat or blocking board for granny squares to block your work (see page 17).

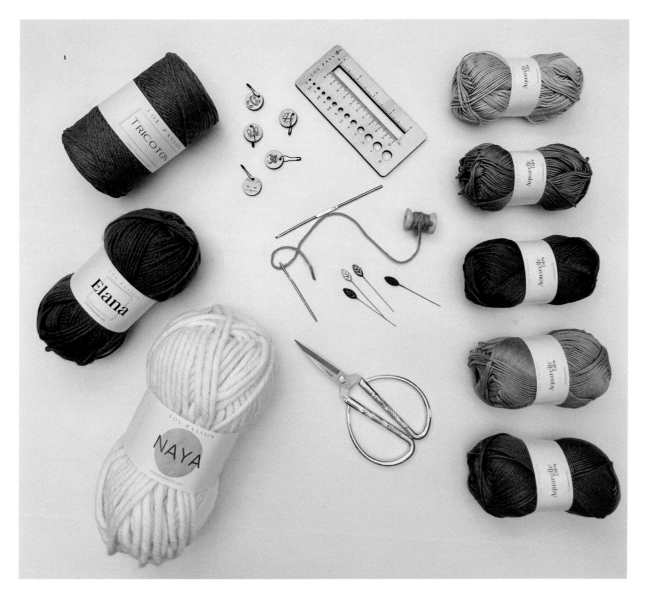

Crochet Techniques

Even though you're new to crochet, you'll quickly learn these concepts as you practice. Start by making small, simple projects that will allow you to practice and quickly develop your skills and techniques.

Getting Started

HOLDING THE CROCHET HOOK

Depending on what suits you best, you can hold your hook like a pen (1) or a knife (2). Regardless of which of the two you prefer and find more comfortable, the result will be the same.

You'll hold the hook with your right hand if you're right-handed or your left hand if you're left-handed. That will influence the direction in which you work. A right-handed person will crochet from right to left, while a left-handed person will crochet from left to right. In this book, we'll demonstrate by crocheting from right to left.

Holding your crochet hook like a pen

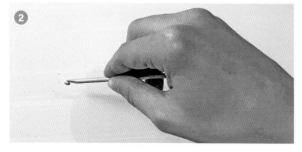

Holding your crochet hook like a knife

No matter which hand you prefer, keep a distance of about 1 to 1.5 inches (3 to 4 cm) between your thumb and the tip of the hook.

HOLDING THE YARN

The loose end of the yarn is called the tail. When making basic stitches, which you do on the right-hand side for right-handers and on the left-hand side for left-handers, you move away from the tail as you work toward the yarn leading to the ball.

Hold the working (being crocheted) yarn with your left hand if you're right-handed, or with your right hand if you're left-handed. Your hook should be between the hand holding the yarn leading to the ball and the yarn tail.

The working yarn should be held taut by at least the index finger of the hand holding it and should remain loose enough to follow the movement of the hook without difficulty. Depending on the tension of the yarn, you will be crocheting more or less tightly. The finished size and the suppleness of your project will depend on the tension, as will its opacity: if you crochet tightly, it will be smaller and stiffer than desired, whereas if you crochet too loosely, it may be too airy and lack hold. You can then adapt your material to obtain the desired result (see box opposite).

The most important thing is to maintain an even tension throughout the work, for an even finish. Similarly, if you're making several squares to be sewn together, it's important that they be of the same consistency for a harmonious result.

Tips on Tension

There's no right or wrong tension. The right tension depends on each individual, and it's by knowing your tension that you'll be able to adjust your work. For example, if you crochet tightly and get a square that's too small and stiff with the recommended yarn and hook, then use a hook that's half a size larger than the yarn label recommends. On the other hand, if you tend to crochet loosely and your square is too large and open-worked for what you need, opt for a hook half a size smaller than the one indicated.

You need to be comfortable. If you want to take up crochet, it's to enjoy some passion, to relax, to escape . . . So *do* relax and don't tense up your fingers and wrist.

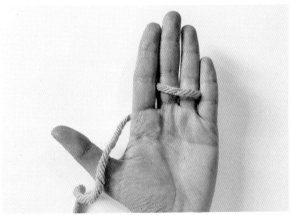

Holding the yarn (option 1)

Holding the yarn (option 2)

THE SLIP KNOT

To start crocheting, first make a slip knot.

1. With the yarn tail heading down and the yarn attached to the ball heading up (see the photo), wrap and cross the yarn around your index and middle fingers (1).

2. Slide the hook head under the upper yarn (2).

3. Grab the yarn with the hook (3) and pull it through the loop (4).

4. Pull gently on the yarn tail (**5**, **6**).

THE MAGIC RING

When crocheting in a circle or spiral, as is the case with granny squares, start by making a magic ring.

Working in a Circle or Spiral

Crocheting in a circle means that each circle is closed with a slip stitch, made in the first stitch of the previous round. The next circle then begins with one or more chain stitches, which never count as a stitch.

And spiral crocheting simply consists of a series of turns *without* closing them with a slip stitch.

1. Make a loop with your hook and yarn, as if you were going to make a slip knot (**1**), but don't pull to close it (**2**).

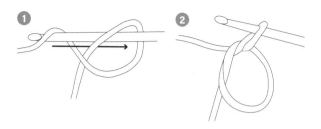

2. Hold the loop between your thumb and middle finger, then wrap the yarn around the tip of the hook (this is called a *yarn over*) and pass it through the loop. You've just made a chain stitch, which counts here as the first stitch of the round (**3**).

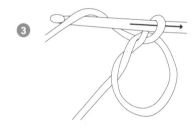

So, if you need to start your first row with three chain stitches, the chain stitch that blocks the magic ring counts as the first of the three. You'll therefore need to do two more chain stitches to reach the total.

3. Make the needed number of chain stitches, working them into the adjustable loop (**4**, **5**, **6**).

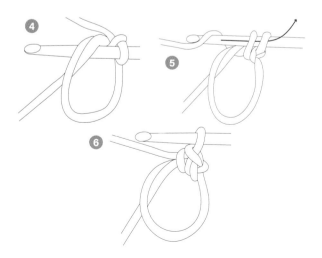

4. Once you've made all your stitches, pull on the shortest end of the yarn (**7**) to close the magic ring (**8**).

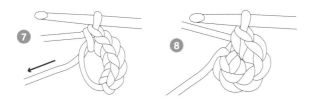

If you're working in a circle rather than in a spiral, close each round with a slip stitch made in the first stitch of the previous round. This means that the next round will begin with one or more chain stitches.

At the end of your work, lock the center of your magic ring with a stitch to keep it tight.

The Stitches

CHAIN STITCH (C.S.)

If you're just starting out, begin by making a slip knot around the hook.

1. Wrap the yarn around the tip of the hook (**1**).

2. Pass the yarn through the loop (**2**). You've now made a chain stitch.

Making a series of chain stitches is simply called "chain stitch."

SLIP STITCH (S.S.)

1. Stitch directly into the crochet stitch (**1**).

At the Start of a Round

If you need to make a slip stitch round, first do a chain stitch, which will not be included in the stitch count, then begin your slip stitch round by stitching into the second stitch from the hook.

2. Place the yarn over the hook and pass the yarn through the two loops (**2**). You've now made a slip stitch.

SINGLE CROCHET

1. Stitch directly into the crochet stitch (**1**).

At the Start of a Round

If you need to make a single crochet stitch round, first create a chain stitch, which will not be included in the stitch count, then begin your single stitch round by stitching into the second stitch from the hook.

2. Work a yarn over and pass the yarn through the stitch; you have two loops on the hook (2).

3. Work a yarn over hook and pass the yarn through the two loops (3). You've now made a single crochet stitch.

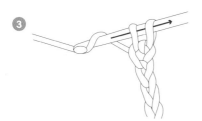

2. Yarn over and pass the yarn through the stitch. You have three loops on the hook (2).

3. Yarn over and pass the yarn through the three loops (3). You've now made a half double crochet stitch.

HALF DOUBLE CROCHET (H.D.C.)

1. Yarn over and stitch in the stitch to be crocheted (1), here in the second chain stitch of the chain.

DOUBLE CROCHET (DC.)

1. Yarn over and stitch in the stitch to be crocheted (1), here in the third chain stitch of the chain.

At the Start of a Round
If you need to make a half double crochet round, first do 2 chain stitches, which will not be included in the stitch count, then begin your half double crochet round by stitching into the 3rd stitch from the hook.

At the Start of a Round
If you need to make a double crochet round, first do 3 chain stitches, which will not be included in the stitch count, then begin your double crochet round by stitching into the 4th stitch from the hook.

2. Yarn over and pass the yarn through the stitch. You have three loops on the hook (**2**).

3. Yarn over and pass the yarn through the two loops. There are two loops left on the hook (**3**).

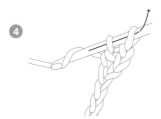

4. Yarn over and pass the yarn through the two loops. (**4**). You've now made a double crochet stitch.

2. Yarn over and pass the yarn through the stitch. You have four loops on the hook (**2**).

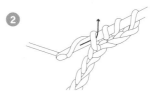

3. Yarn over and pass the yarn through the two loops. There are three loops left on the hook (**3**).

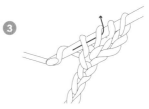

4. Yarn over and pass the yarn through the two loops. There are two loops left on the hook (**4**).

5. Yarn over and pass the yarn through the two loops (**5**). You've now made a triple crochet stitch.

TRIPLE CROCHET (TR.)

1. Yarn over twice and stitch in the stitch to be crocheted (**1**), here in the fifth chain stitch on the chain.

At the Start of a Round
If you need to make a triple crochet round, first make 4 chain stitches, which will not be included in the stitch count, then start your triple crochet round by stitching into the 5th stitch from the hook.

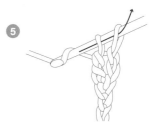

THE PUFF STITCH

The puff stitch is made up of a group of three or five half double crochet folded together in the same stitch. It creates volume.

1. To make a puff stitch of three half double crochet, repeat three times *work a yarn over (1) and stitch into the stitch to be crocheted, yarn over, and pass the yarn through the stitch (2)*.

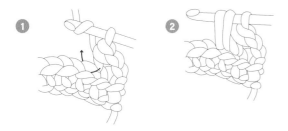

Asterisks

When instructions are enclosed in asterisks, they must be repeated as many times as indicated.

2. Yarn over (3) and pass the yarn through the seven loops (4). You've now made a puff stitch.

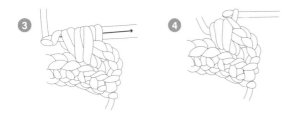

If the instructions say to make a puff stitch of five half double crochets, repeat the steps between asterisks in step 1.

THE BOBBLE STITCH

The bobble stitch is made up of a group of three or five double crochets folded together in the same stitch. It adds texture to the surface.

1. Yarn over and stitch in the stitch to be crocheted (1), in the case in the third chain stitch on the chain, then make another yarn over and pass the yarn through the stitch (2).

2. Yarn over and pass the yarn through the two loops (3). You have two loops on the hook.

3. Still stitching in the same stitch (4), repeat steps 1 and 2 twice for a bobble stitch with triple crochet, or four times for a five stitch bobble stitch. In the first case, you'll have four loops left on the hook; in the second, six.

4. Yarn over and pass the yarn through all the loops (5), then work a last yarn over (6). You've now made a bobble stitch.

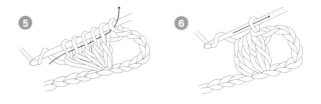

THE PICOT STITCH

The picot stitch is made up of a group of three or five chain stitches. It's used to create a jagged border.

1. From the previous row or round, make a three- or five-stitch chain (**1**).

2. On the chain, starting from the hook, count three or five stitches and stitch into the next stitch (**2**), then make a slip stitch (**3**). You've now made a picot stitch.

Reading a Pattern

In Part 2, you'll find written instructions and a pattern for each square. You can refer to either of these to complete the squares, since both present the same instructions in different ways.

A square's pattern details each stitch made, from the first to the last round. Reading is counterclockwise for right-handers, and clockwise for left-handers.

Each round begins at the same point, usually with chain stitches in the case of squares. This is also where you attach the new yarn when there's a change of color.

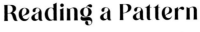

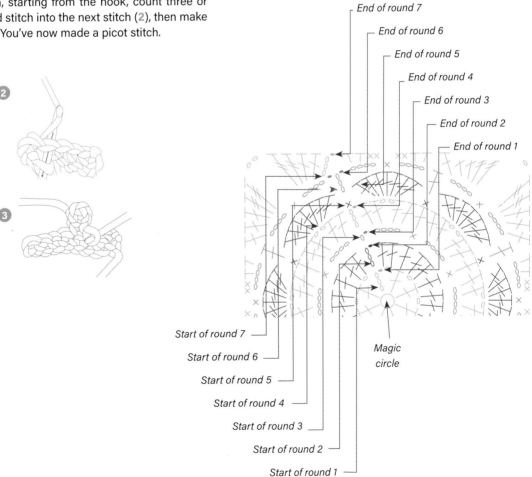

When crocheting in rows—for example, to turn the square into a pillow cover (see page 93)—the pattern should be read from bottom to top and from right to left. At the end of the row, simply turn the square to start the next row.

KEY TO SYMBOLS	
◯	Magic ring
◦	Chain stitch (c.s.)
•	Slip stitch (s.s.)
×	Single crochet (s.c.)
T	Half double crochet (h.d.c.)
⊤	Double crochet (dc.)
⊤	Triple crochet (tr.)
⬭	Puff stitch with three half double crochets
⬭	Puff stitch with five half double crochets
⬦	Three stitch bobble stitch
⬦	Five stitch bobble stitch
⬭	Five chain picot stitch

Changing Yarns or Colors

When you reach the end of your yarn ball or need to change color (which is often the case when making granny squares), you need to discreetly attach a new yarn to the work.

Tip
It's always best to change yarn at the end of a round for a more subtle transition. So, if you don't think you have enough yarn left to complete a new round, attach the new yarn before you start it.

1. Make a chain stitch to fasten off the current yarn. Cut it off, leaving about 4 inches to weave it in afterward, then pull the yarn through the loop.

At the Start of a Round
This chain stitch does not count as the first stitch for the new row, unless you're making a row, which will start with three chain stitches.

So, for your row, the chain stitch that blocks the new yarn counts as the first of the three to be made, so you'll need to make two more to reach the total.

2. Using the new yarn, stitch into the first stitch of the previous row and yarn over.

3. Bring the loop back through the stitch.

4. Make a chain stitch to **block** the new yarn.

Finishing

FASTENING OFF YARN ENDS

If you want to change color or if you have finished a section, you need to fasten off your yarn.

1. At the end of the last round, make a slip stitch by stitching into the initial round stitch. You can also work a chain stitch afterward.

2. Cut the yarn to a length of about 6 inches, then pull the yarn through the loop.

WEAVING IN YARN ENDS

It's very important to weave the yarn ends in carefully to achieve a beautiful finish and ensure that your work lasts over time.

1. Using a yarn needle and on the back side of the piece, stitch through the stitches of the last round to bring the yarn through.

2. Then cut the yarn end short.

BLOCKING

In crochet, blocking involves washing the crocheted piece and pinning it to a support to shape it so that it dries to the right dimensions.

This is even more important in the case of geometric shapes such as granny squares. Each square in the same project must be blocked to the right size before being sewn to the others; otherwise you'll have trouble sewing them edge to edge and getting an aesthetically pleasing result.

To block a granny square you'll need:

- Pins.
- A padded board on which to pin the squares, or a blocking board (a wooden support with holes and pins).
- A container the size of the square.
- Delicate/wool detergent or shampoo.
- A towel.

1. Soak the square for at least two hours in a container of cold water with a little wool detergent (1).

2. Wring the granny square out (2), then place it in a towel and twist a little so that the towel absorbs the water from the square.

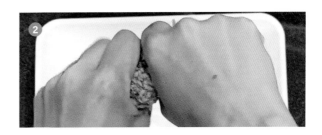

3. On your board, pin the corners of the square to the desired dimensions. Make sure that all the sides are the same length, to obtain a nice square (3), and let it dry.

Careful!

When you're crocheting multiple squares for one project, make sure that the squares' dimensions are identical.

JOINING SQUARES

There are various techniques for connecting your crochet squares. Not only does joining allow you to sew the pieces together to create a project, but the seam also adds a nice finishing touch, which differs according to the technique.

A visible seam is sewn on the front of the pieces, while an invisible seam is sewn on the back. The right-hand side of a round or spiral stitch is the part that faces you when you crochet. If necessary, insert a marker on the right-hand side of your squares to make it easier to locate. This is especially helpful when you need to join several squares in a row. For discreet stitching, use a yarn of the same color as the last round of the squares to be joined.

To join two squares together almost invisibly with a yarn needle, place them right sides together and match up the edges, then join them stitch by stitch in one of these ways:

By stitching only into the back loops of the two squares (A). With the needle technique, the result (B) is tighter than crocheted seams.

Front Loops and Back Loops

To recognize a front or back loop, look at your stitches from above. They form a "V": the front loop corresponds to the part of the V closest to you (in blue), while the back loop corresponds to the part farthest from you (in yellow).

To join two squares seamlessly with the crochet hook, place them right sides together and match up the edges, then join them stitch by stitch:

- With slip stitch or single crochet stitches, stitching only into the back loops of the two squares (A). Both methods offer a discreet and flexible finish (B).

- Or by stitching under a chain and directly into a stitch; for example, by stitching into a double crochet (C). This option creates a small raised area on the back of the work, but the seam is less visible than other methods (D).

For the corners of the squares, stitch either in the **loop created by the chain stitches, or in the back loop of the chain stitches.**

The visible seams are made on the right side of the pieces (E), in the front or back loops, and the squares must then be placed wrong sides together before being joined. The result will vary depending on whether you're using slip stitches or single crochet stitches (F). The single crochet stitches create a more pronounced texture, which you might find useful for accessories such as bags.

- Or with slip stitch or single crochet stitches, stitching only into the front loops (C). The result is a little tighter than with the previous methods (D).

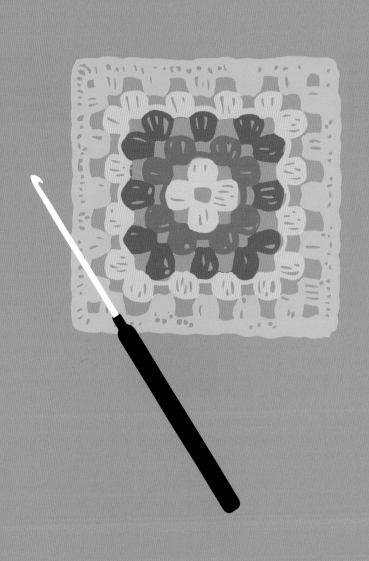

PART 2

Crocheting the Squares

Granny Square

This square is a classic, the simplest and most representative
design of what granny squares are all about.
It's easy to make and easy to adapt.

MATERIALS

3 mm crochet hook
Yarn Used: Aquarelle
(see page 6 for substitution info)
- coral (320)
- terracotta (190)
- mustard (900)

DIMENSIONS

2.5" × 2.5" (6.5 × 6.5 cm)

STITCHES USED

Magic ring (page 10)
Chain stitch (page 11)
Slip stitch (page 11)
Double crochet (page 12)

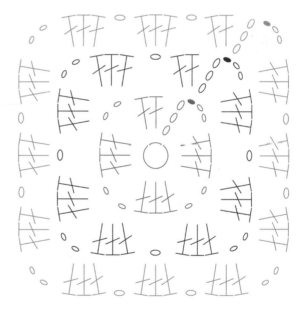

ROUND 1

With the coral yarn, make a magic ring, then 3 c.s. (that will count as the first double crochet), 2 dc. in the ring, 2 c.s.

Still in the ring, repeat 3 times *3 dc., 2 c.s.*. Pull on the yarn tail to close the ring.

Finish with 1 s.s. in the 3rd initial c.s. of the turn, then fasten off.

ROUND 2

Attach the terracotta yarn to the starting corner with 1 s.s., make 3 c.s. (that will count as the first double crochet) and 2 dc. at the same angle, then 1 c.s.

Repeat 3 times *[3 dc., 2 c.s., 3 dc.] in each corner, 1 c.s.*.

Make 3 dc. in the starting angle, 2 c.s., 1 s.s. in the 3rd initial chain stitch of the turn, then fasten off.

ROUND 3

Attach mustard yarn to starting corner with

1 s.s., make 3 c.s. (which count as the 1st double crochet) and

2 dc. in the same corner, then 1 c.s. In the next space, do 3 dc., 1 c.s.

Repeat 3 times *[3 dc., 2 c.s., 3 dc.] in corner, 1 c.s., 3 dc. in next space, 1 c.s.*.

Do 3 dc. in the starting corner, 2 c.s., 1 s.s. in the 3rd initial c.s. of the turn, then fasten off.

Full Square

A variation on the traditional granny square, this design has less openwork and is just as easy to make. It allows you to create denser, warmer projects.

MATERIALS

2.5 mm crochet hook
Yarn Used: Aquarelle
(see page 6 for substitution info)
- horizon blue (515)
- navy blue (535)
- bottle green (725)

DIMENSIONS

2.75" × 2.75" (7 × 7 cm)

STITCHES USED

Magic ring (page 10)
Chain stitch (page 11)
Slip stitch (page 11)
Double crochet (page 12)

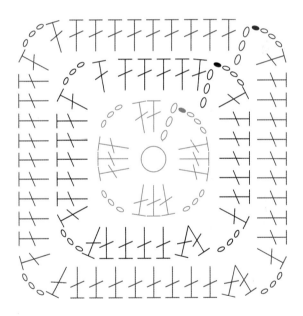

ROUND 1

With the horizon-blue yarn, make a magic ring, then 3 c.s. (counting as 1st double crochet), 2 dc. in the ring, 3 c.s.

Still in the ring, repeat 3 times *3 dc., 3 c.s.*. Pull on the yarn tail to close the circle.

Finish with 1 s.s. in the 3rd initial c.s. of the turn, then fasten off.

ROUND 2

With the navy-blue yarn, stitch in the last chain stitch of the previous turn, make 3 c.s. (which count for 1st double crochet), 1 dc., then 1 dc. in the next 3 stitches.

Repeat 3 times *[2 dc., 3 c.s., 2 dc.] in the corner, 1 dc. in the next 3 stitches*.

Make 2 dc. in the starting corner, 3 c.s., 1 s.s. in the 3rd initial c.s. of the round, then fasten off.

ROUND 3

Attach the bottle-green yarn to the starting corner with 1 s.s., make 3 c.s. (which count as 1st double crochet), 1 dc. then 1 dc. in the next 7 stitches.

Repeat 3 times *[2 dc., 3 c.s., 2 dc.] in the corner, 1 dc. in the next 7 stitches*.

Make 2 dc. in the starting corner, 3 c.s., 1 dc. in the 3rd initial c.s. of the round, then fasten off.

Circle Square

This design incorporates a circle into the traditional granny square, adding roundness and giving the center a flared look. Create subtly shaded and modern-feeling projects by playing with its colors.

———

MATERIALS

2.5 mm crochet hook
Yarn Used: Aquarelle
(see page 6 for substitution info)
- navy blue (535)
- terracotta (190)
- coral (320)

DIMENSIONS

3" × 3" (8.5 × 8.5 cm)

STITCHES USED

Magic ring (page 10)
Chain stitch (page 11)
Slip stitch (page 11)
Double crochet (page 12)

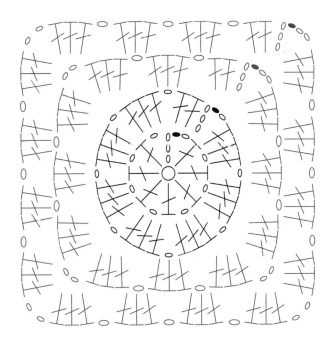

ROUND 1

With the navy-blue yarn make a magic ring, then 3 c.s. (counting for the 1st double crochet) and 1 c.s. still in the ring, repeat 7 times *1 dc., 1 c.s.*. Pull on the yarn tail to close the circle.

Finish with 1 s.s. in the 3rd initial chain stitch of the loop.

ROUND 2

Still using the navy-blue yarn, make 1 s.s. to position yourself between the 2 dc. of the previous turn, then 3 c.s. (counting for the 1st dc.), 2 dc. in the same starting space, 1 c.s.

Repeat 7 times *[3 dc., 1 c.s.] in the space between 2 dc. of the previous turn*.

Finish with 1 s.s. in the 3rd initial c.s. of the turn, then fasten off.

ROUND 3

Attach the terracotta yarn in the space formed by the last chain stitch of the previous turn with 1 s.s., make 3 c.s. (which count as the 1st double crochet), 2 dc. in the same starting space, 1 c.s.

In the next space, do 3 dc., 1 c.s.

Repeat 3 times *[3 dc., 2 c.s., 3 dc.] in next space, 1 c.s., 3 dc. in next space, 1 c.s.*.

Make 3 dc. in the starting space of the turn, 2 c.s., 1 s.s. in the 3rd initial c.s. of the turn, then fasten off.

ROUND 4

Attach the coral yarn to the starting angle with 1 slip stitch, make 3 c.s. (which count as the 1st double crochet) and 2 dc. in the same corner, 1 c.s.. In each of the next two spaces, do 3 dc., 1 c.s.

Repeat 3 times *[3 dc., 2 c.s., 3 dc.] in the corner, 1 c.s., [3 dc., 1 c.s.] in each of the next two spaces*.

Make 3 dc. in the starting corner, 2 c.s., 1 s.s. in the 3rd initial c.s. of the turn, then fasten off.

Flower Square

This soft, dense square is especially ideal for decorative projects such as pillows, baskets, and rugs.

MATERIALS

3 mm crochet hook
Yarn Used: Elana
(see page 6 for substitution info)
- mustard (742)
- Esmeralda (652)
- bottle green (611)

DIMENSIONS

3" × 3" (7.5 × 7.5 cm)

STITCHES USED

Magic ring (page 10)
Chain stitch (page 11)
Slip stitch (page 11)
Single crochet (page 11)
Half double crochet (page 12)
Double crochet (page 12)
Three-stitch bobble stitch
(page 14)

ROUND 1

With the mustard yarn, make a magic ring, then 1 three stitch bobble stitch in the ring (replacing the 1st dc. of the stitch with 2 c.s.), 1 s.s.

Still in the ring, repeat 7 times *1 bobble stitch, 1 c.s.

Pull yarn tail to close circle.

Finish with 1 slip stitch in the 2nd chain stitch of the 1st bobble stitch of the round, then fasten off.

ROUND 2

Attach the Esmeralda yarn between the first and last bobble stitches of the previous round with 1 s.s., do [1 bobble stitch (replacing the 1st dc. of the stitch with 2 c.s.), 1 c.s., 1 bobble stitch] in the same starting space, 1 c.s.

Repeat 7 times *[1 bobble stitch, 1 chain stitch, 1 bobble stitch] in the next space, 1 chain stitch*.

Finish with 1 slip stitch in the 2nd chain stitch of the 1st bobble stitch of the round, then fasten off.

ROUND 3

Attach the bottle-green yarn between the first and last group of 2 bobble stitches from the previous round with 1 s.s., make 3 chain stitch (which count for the 1st dc.), 2 dc. in the same starting space.

Do 3 half double crochets in the next space, 3 single crochets in the one after and 3 hdc. in the one after that.

Repeat 3 times *[3 dc., 2 c.s., 3 dc.] in the next space, 3 hdc. in the next space, 3 s.c. in the next space, 3 hdc. in the next space*.

Finish with 1 s.s. in the 3rd initial chain stitch of the turn, then fasten off.

Soft Square

Here's an unusual take on the traditional granny square.
Lightweight and easy to make, it's ideal for creating fashion accessories
such as bags, belts, headbands, and more.

MATERIALS

2.5 mm crochet hook
Yarn Used: Aquarelle
(see page 6 for substitution info)
- chestnut (30)
- terracotta (190)
- mustard (900)

DIMENSIONS

2.25" × 2.25" (6 × 6 cm)

STITCHES USED

Magic ring (page 10)
Chain stitch (page 11)
Slip stitch (page 11)
Single crochet (page 11)
Double crochet (page 12)
Puff stitch with three half
double crochets (page 14)

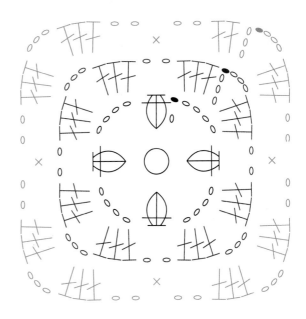

ROUND 1

With the chestnut yarn, make a magic ring, 1 c.s. Repeat 4 times *1 puff stitch in the ring, 4 c.s.*. Pull on the tail to close the circle.

Finish with 1 s.s. in the top stitch of the round's 1st puff stitch, then fasten off.

ROUND 2

Attach the terracotta yarn to the starting angle with 1 s.s., make 3 c.s. (counts as 1st double crochet), 2 double crochets in same angle, 2 c.s.

Repeat in each corner *[3 double crochets, 3 chain stitches, 3 double crochets], 2 c.s*.

Make 3 dc. in the starting angle, 3 c.s., 1 s.s. in the 3rd initial chain stitch of the turn, then end the yarn.

ROUND 3

Attach the mustard yarn to the starting corner with 1 s.s., make 3 c.s. (which count as the 1st double crochet) and 2 dc. at the same angle, 2 c.s.

Repeat 3 times *1 s.s. in the next space, 2 c.s., [3 double crochets, 3 chain stitches, double crochets] in the corner, 2 c.s., 1 s.c. in the next space, 2 c.s*.

Make 3 dc. in the starting corner, 3 c.s., 1 s.s. in the 3rd initial c.s. of the turn, then end the yarn.

Emmy Square

This original and easy-to-crochet pattern is a wonderful addition to your square repertoire, bringing a touch of elegance to projects.

MATERIALS

3 mm crochet hook
Yarn Used: Emmy
(see page 6 for substitution info)
- asparagus green (35)
  - yellow (28)
    - gray (44)
  - cream (23)

DIMENSIONS

4.25" × 4.25" (11 × 11 cm)

STITCHES USED

Magic ring (page 10)
Chain stitch (page 11)
Slip stitch (page 11)
Single crochet (page 11)
Double crochet (page 12)
Five-chain picot stitch
(page 15)

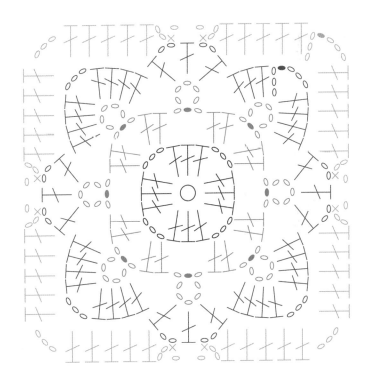

ROUND 1

With the asparagus-green yarn, make a magic ring, 3 c.s. (which count as 1st double crochet), 2 dc. in the ring, 3 c.s.

Repeat 3 times *3 c.s. in the ring, 3 c.s.*. Pull tail to close ring.

Finish with 1 s.s. in the 3rd initial c.s. of the turn, then fasten off.

ROUND 2

Attach the yellow yarn to the starting angle with 1 s.s., make 3 c.s. (counts as 1st dc.), 1 dc. in same angle, 6 c.s., 1 picot with 1 s.s. in 5th dc. from hook, 1 c.s.

Repeat 3 times *2 dc. in the next angle, 6 c.s., 1 picot stitch 1 s.s. in the 5th chain stitch from the hook, 1 c.s. in the next angle from hook, 1 dc., 2 dc. in same angle, 6 dc., 1 picot with 1 s.s. in 5th double crochet from hook, 1 dc.*.

Make 2 dc. in the starting angle, 6 dc., 1 picot with 1 s.s. in the 5th dc. from the hook, 1 dc., 1 s.s. in the initial 3rd c.s. of the turn, then fasten off.

ROUND 3

Attach the gray yarn to the starting corner picot with 1 s.s., make 3 c.s. (which count as 1st double crochet), 3 strands in the same picot.

In the next picot, make 1 dc., 2 c.s., 1 dc., 2 c.s., 1 dc..

Repeat 3 times *[4 dc., 3 c.s., 4 dc.] in the corner picot, [1 dc., 2 c.s., 1 dc., 2 c.s., 1 dc.] in the next picot*.

Make 4 dc. in the initial picot of the round, 3 chain stitches, 1 s.s. in the 3rd initial c.s. of the round, then fasten off.

ROUND 4

Attach the cream yarn to the starting corner with 1 s.s., make 3 c.s. (which count as 1st double crochet) and 1 dc. in the same angle.

Repeat 3 times *1 dc. in the next 4 stitches, 2 c.s., 1 s.c. in the loop created by the 2 c.s., 2 c.s., 1 s.c. in the loop formed by the 2 c.s., 2 c.s., 1 dc. in the next 4 meshes, [2 dc., 3 chain stitches, 2 dc.] in the corner*.

Make 1 dc. in the next 4 meshes, 2 c.s., 1 s.s. in the loop created by the 2 c.s., 2 c.s., 1 s.s. in the loop created by the 2 c.s. 2 c.s., 1 dc. in the following 4 meshes.

Make 2 dc. in the starting angle, 3 c.s., 1 s.s. in the 3rd initial c.s. of the turn, then fasten off.

Puff Square

This design is a granny square staple. It combines the classic Full Square and the textured look of the Flower Square.

MATERIALS

2.5 mm crochet hook
Yarn Used: Aquarelle
(see page 6 for substitution info)
- mustard (900)
- old pink (40)
- coral (320)
- tan (300)

DIMENSIONS

3.25" × 3.25" (8.5 × 8.5 cm)

STITCHES USED

Magic ring (page 10)
Chain stitch (page 11)
Slip stitch (page 11)
Double crochet (page 12)
Puff stitch with three half
double crochets (page 14)

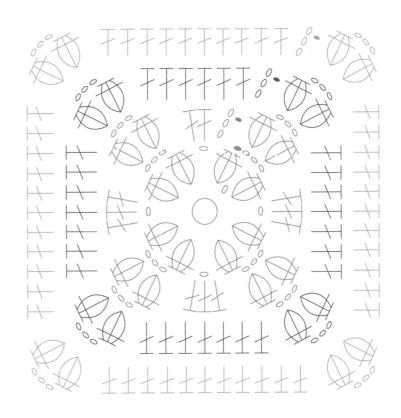

ROUND 1

With the mustard yarn, make a magic ring, 1 chain stitch, then repeat 4 times *[1 puff stitch, 1 c.s., 1 puff stitch] in the circle, 3 chain stitches*.

Pull on the yarn tail to close the circle.

Finish with 1 slip stitch in the stitch of the 1st puff stitch of the round, then fasten off.

ROUND 2

Attach the old-pink yarn in the space between the 1st and 2nd puff stitch of the previous turn with 1 s.s., make 3 c.s. (which count as 1st double crochet), 2 dc. in the same space.

Repeat 3 times *[1 puff stitch, 3 chain stitches, 1 puff stitch] in the next 3 c.s. loop, 3 dc. in the next 1 c.s. loop*.

In the last loop, make all of the following [1 puff stitch, 3 chain stitches, 1 puff stitch].

Finish with 1 slip stitch in the 3rd initial c.s. of the turn, then fasten off.

ROUND 3

Attach the coral yarn between the first trio of dc. and the last puff stitch of the previous round with I s.s., make 3 c.s. (which count as 1st dc.) and 1 dc. in the same starting space.

Make 1 dc. in the next 3 stitches, 2 dc. between the next dc. trio and the following puff stitch.

Repeat 3 times *[1 puff stitch, 3 chain stitch, 1 puff stitch] in the corner, 2 dc. between 1 puff stitch and a trio of dc., 1 dc. in the next 3 meshes, 2 dc. between a trio of dc. and 1 puff stitch*.

In the last corner, make 1 puff stitch, 3 c.s., 1 puff stitch.

Finish with 1 slip stitch in the initial 3rd c.s. of the turn, then fasten off.

ROUND 4

Attach the yarn between 1 puff stitch and a group of 2 dc. with 1 s.s., make 3 c.s. (which count as the 1st dc.), 1 dc. in the same starting space.

Make 1 dc. in the next 7 stitches, 2 dc. between the group of 2 dc. and 1 puff stitch from the previous round.

Repeat 3 times *[1 puff stitch, 3 c.s., 1 puff stitch] in the corner, 2 dc. between 1 puff stitch and a group of 2 dc. from the previous round, 1 dc. in the next 7 meshes, 2 dc. between a group of 2 dc. and 1 puff stitch from the previous round*.

In the last corner, do 1 puff stitch, 3 c.s., 1 puff stitch.

Finish with 1 s.s. in the initial 3rd c.s. of the round, then fasten off.

Sunflower Square

This dense, textured square is ideal for so many projects and works especially wonderfully in garments and accessories.

———

MATERIALS

2.5 mm crochet hook
Yarn Used: Aquarelle
(see page 6 for substitution info)
- bottle green (725)
- sage (612)
- mustard (900)
- gray (819)

DIMENSIONS

3.25" × 3.25" (8 × 8 cm)

STITCHES USED

Magic ring (page 10)
Chain stitch (page 11)
Slip stitch (page 11)
Double crochet (page 12)
Puff stitch with five half double crochets (page 14)
Five-stitch bobble stitch (page 14)

ROUND 1

With the bottle-green yarn, make a magic ring, then 3 c.s. (which counts as the 1st double crochet), 1 chain stitch.

Repeat 15 times *1 dc. in circle, 1 chain stitch.*. Pull on the yarn tail to close the circle.

Finish with 1 s.s. in the 3rd initial chain stitch of the turn, then fasten off.

ROUND 2

Attach the sage yarn between the first two strands of the previous round with 1 s.s., do 1 c.s.

Repeat 16 times *1 stitch in the space created by the c.s. of the previous round, 1 c.s*.

Finish with 1 slip stitch in the stitch of the 1st puff of the round, then fasten off.

ROUND 3

Attach the mustard yarn in the space created by the last stitch of the previous round with 1 s.s., do 1 s.s., then repeat 16 times *1 puff stitch in the next space, 1 c.s*.

Finish with 1 s.s. in the stitch of the 1st puff stitch of the round, then fasten off.

ROUND 4

Attach the gray yarn in the space created by the last chain stitch of the previous turn with 1 s.s., make 3 c.s. (which count as the 1st dc.), 2 dc. in the same starting space.

Repeat 3 times *3 dc. in the next space*.

Repeat 3 times *[3 dc., 2 chain stitches, 3 dc.] in next space, 3 dc. in next space, 3 dc. in next space, 3 dc. in next space*.

Do 3 dc. in the starting space, 2 c.s., 1 s.s. in the 3rd initial chain stitch of the turn, then end the yarn.

Magalie Square

Halfway between the traditional Granny Square and the Circle Square, this design is elegant and easy to make. Try it for projects like stoles or lightweight jackets.

—

MATERIALS

2.5 mm crochet hook
Yarn Used: Aquarelle
(see page 6 for substitution info)
- chestnut (30)
- bottle green (725)
- horizon blue (515)

DIMENSIONS

4.25" × 4.25" (11 × 11 cm)

STITCHES USED

Magic ring (page 10)
Chain stitch (page 11)
Slip stitch (page 11)
Double crochet (page 12)
Triple crochet (page 13)

ROUND 1

With the chestnut yarn, make a magic ring, then 3 c.s. (counts as 1st double crochet), 1 c.s.

Repeat 11 times *1 dc. in the ring, 1 c.s.*. Pull on the yarn tail to close the ring.

Finish with 1 s.s. in the 3rd initial c.s. of the turn, then fasten off.

ROUND 2

Attach the bottle-green yarn in the space created by the last c.s. of the previous turn with 1 s.s, make 3 c.s. (which count as the 1st double crochet), 1 strand in the same starting space, 1 c.s.

Repeat 11 times *2 dc. in the space created by the c.s., 1 c.s.*.

Finish with 1 s.s. in the 3rd initial chain stitch of the turn, then fasten off.

ROUND 3

Attach the bottle-green yarn between the first and last groups of dc. of the previous round with 1 s.s., make 3 c.s. (counts as 1st double crochet), 2 dc. in same starting space, 1 c.s.

Repeat 11 times *3 dc. in next space, 1 c.s.*.

Finish with 1 s.s. in the 3rd initial chain stitch of the turn, then fasten off.

ROUND 4

Attach the horizon-blue yarn between the first and last groups of double crochets of the previous round with 1 s.s., make 4 c.s. (counts as 1st triple crochet), 2 triple crochets in same starting space, 1 c.s.

Repeat 2 times *3 double crochets in the next space, 1 c.s.*.

Repeat 3 times *[3 triple crochets, 3 c.s., 3 triple crochets] in next space, 1 c.s., 3 double crochets in next space, 1 c.s., 3 dc. in next space, 1 c.s.*.

Make 3 triple crochets in the starting space, 3 c.s., 1 s.s. in the 4th initial c.s. of the turn, then fasten off.

ROUND 5

Still using the horizon-blue yarn, make 3 c.s. (counting for the 1st double crochet), 1 dc. in the same starting space.

Make 1 dc. in the next 15 stitches.

Repeat 3 times *[2 double crochets, 2 chain stitches, 2 double crochets] in the corner, 1 dc. in the next 15 stitches*.

Make 2 dc. in the starting corner, 2 c.s., 1 s.s. in the 3rd initial chain stitch of the round, then fasten off.

Boho Square

This unusual easy-to-make square is shaped like a flower. Its chic, bohemian curves look great in a wide range of colors.

MATERIALS

3 mm crochet hook
Yarn Used: Elana
(see page 6 for substitution info)
- mustard (742)
- navy blue (552)
- light blue (640)

DIMENSIONS

5.25" × 5.25" (13.5 × 13.5 cm)

STITCHES USED

Magic ring (page 10)
Chain stitch (page 11)
Slip stitch (page 11)
Single crochet (page 11)
Half double crochet (page 12)
Double crochet (page 12)
Triple crochet (page 13)

ROUND 1

With the mustard yarn, make a magic ring, 3 c.s. (counts as 1st double crochet), 1 c.s.

Repeat 7 times *1 dc. in the ring, 1 c.s.*. Pull tail to close the ring.

Finish with 1 s.s. in the 3rd initial c.s. of the turn, then end the yarn.

ROUND 2

Attach the navy-blue yarn to the 1st stitch of the previous round with 1 dc., make 3 c.s. (counts as 1st double crochet), 2 dc. in next space.

Repeat 7 times *1 dc. in next stitch, 2 dc. in next space*.

Finish with 1 s.s. in the 3rd initial c.s. of the turn, then fasten off.

ROUND 3

Attach the blue mineral yarn to the 1st stitch of the previous round with 1 s.s., make 1 c.s. (which counts as the 1st double crochet), 4 c.s.

Repeat 7 times *skip 2 stitches, 1 s.c., 4 c.s.*.

Finish with 1 s.s. in the 1st s.c. of the round, then fasten off.

ROUND 4

Attach the mustard yarn to the 1st stitch of the previous round with 1 s.s., make 3 c.s. (which count as 1st dc.), [2 dc., 2 c.s., 2 dc.] in the loop created by the c.s. from the previous round.

Repeat 7 times *1 dc. in the single crochet, [2 double crochets, 2 c.s., 2 dc.] in the loop created by the chain stitch*.

Finish with 1 s.s. in the 3rd initial c.s. of the turn, then fasten off.

ROUND 5

Attach the navy-blue yarn to the 1st stitch of the previous round with 1 s.s., make 1 c.s. (which counts as the 1st single crochet), 7 dc. in the next space created by the c.s. of previous round, then skip 2 stitches.

Repeat 7 times *1 s.c., 7 dc. in the space created by the c.s., skip 2 stitches*.

Finish with 1 s.s. in the 1st s.c. of the round, then fasten off.

ROUND 6

Attach the light-blue yarn to the 1st stitch of the previous round with 1 s.s., do 3 c.s. (that count as 1st double crochet) 4 s.c., then skip 3 stitches, do 1 s.c., 4 c.s. and skip 3 stitches.

Repeat 7 times *1 dc., 4 c.s., skip 3 stitches, 1 s.c., 4 c.s., skip 3 stitches*.

Finish with 1 s.s. in the initial 3rd c.s. of the round, then fasten off.

ROUND 7

Attach the mustard yarn just after the 1st dc. of the previous turn with 1 s.s., make 3 c.s. (which count as 1st dc.), [2 dc., 2 triple crochets] in the same starting space, 2 c.s.

Then do [2 triple crochets, 3 dc.] in the next space, [2 h.d.c., 2 s.s.] in the next space, [2 s.s., 2 h.d.c.] in the next space.

Repeat 3 times *[3 dc., 2 triple crochets] in the next space, 2 c.s., [2 h.d.c., 3 dc.] in the next space, [2 h.d.c, 2 s.s.] in the next space, [2 s.s., 2 h.d.c] in the next space*.

Finish with 1 s.s. in the initial 3rd c.s. of the round, then fasten off.

PART 3

Making the Projects

Belt

TIME NEEDED:
About 3 hours

Add pizzazz to any outfit with this lovely belt. Choose squares to give it a unique pattern, and match its colors to your favorite dresses and tunics. This project is ideal for getting started!

MATERIALS

3 mm crochet hook
Yarn Used: Aquarelle
(see page 6 for substitution info)
- old pink (40), 1 ball
- terracotta (190), 1 ball
- coral (320), 1 ball
- mustard (900), 1 ball

DIMENSIONS

1 square: 2.5" × 2.5"
(6.5 × 6.5 cm)
Belt (without ties): 31.5"
(80 cm) (size S) to 54"
(138 cm) (size 6XL)

STITCHES USED

Magic ring (page 10)
Chain stitch (page 11)
Slip stitch (page 11)
Double crochet (page 12)

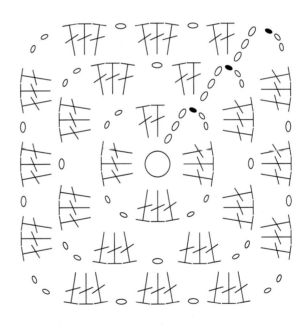

GRANNY SQUARE

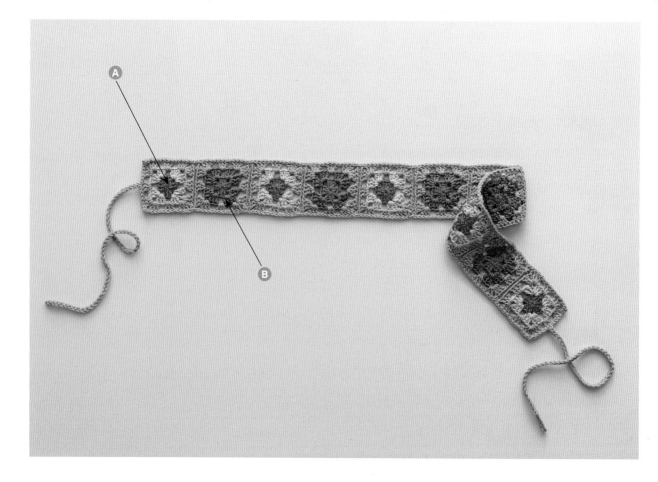

Squares

Refer to the sizes on the opposite page for the
number of granny squares to crochet
(see instructions on page 23), alternating the
different yarn colors.

VERSION A

Round 1: coral
Round 2: old pink
Round 3: mustard

VERSION B

Round 1: coral
Round 2: terracotta
Round 3: mustard

Number of Squares, by Belt Size

XS: repeat versions A and B 6 times.

S: repeat version A 7 times; repeat version B 6 times.

M: repeat versions A and B 7 times.

L: repeat version A 8 times; repeat version B 7 times.

XL: repeat versions A and B 8 times.

2XL: repeat version A 9 times; repeat version B 8 times.

3XL: repeat versions A and B 9 times.

4XL: repeat versions A 10 times; repeat version B 9 times.

5XL: repeat versions A and B 10 times.

6XL: repeat versions A 11 times; repeat version B 10 times.

Tip

If you want to customize the belt's size before crocheting the border, hold the joined row of squares lightly around your waist to check that it's the correct length.

Instructions

JOINING THE SQUARES

When all the squares are crocheted and blocked and their ends are woven in, begin joining with the mustard yarn.

Join the squares together by crocheting slip stitches into the back loops of the squares (see page 18).

1. Place square A and square B right sides together.

2. Attach the yarn to the chain stitches at the angle of squares A and B with 1 slip stitch: hook into the chain stitches of both squares at the same time, as if they were a single stitch.

3. Crochet 13 slip stitches, always stitching into the back loops of both squares.

4. Repeat for the following squares, alternating A and B versions.

BORDER AND TIES

The border and the two ties at the ends of the belt are made in one piece by going around the band of joined squares.

1. Tie the mustard yarn to one of the squares at the end of the band, making 1 slip stitch just before the center break of the square.

2. Crochet a chain of 61 chain stitches, or the number of stitches needed to achieve the desired strap length.

3. Make 1 slip stitch in every stitch of the chain, starting with the 2nd chain stitch from the hook, to form the first strap.

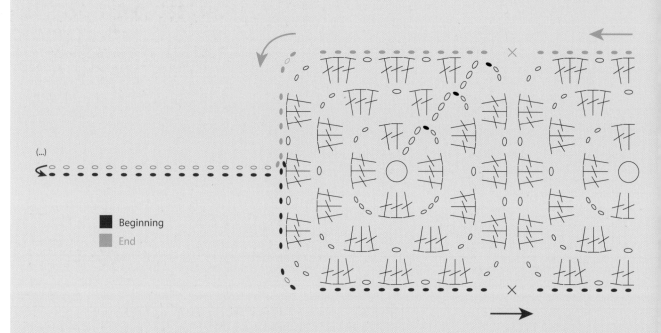

■ Beginning
■ End

4. Then crochet 1 slip stitch in the middle dc. on the square, 5 slip stitches in the next stitches, then 1 slip stitch, 1 chain stitch, 1 slip stitch in the corner stitches.

5. Repeat *1 slip stitch in each stitch of a square, 1 single crochet where two squares join* along the length of the belt to the corner of the last square and hook 1 slip stitch, 1 chain stitch, 1 slip stitch, then 6 slip stitches on the side.

6. Make a new chain of 61 chain stitches, or the number of stitches crocheted for the first strap.

7. Make 1 slip stitch in every stitch of the chain, starting in the second chain stitch from the hook, to form the second strap.

8. Then crochet 1 slip stitch in the middle double crochet on the square, 5 slip stitches in the next stitches, then 1 slip stitch, 1 chain stitch, 1 slip stitch in the corner stitches.

9. Continue on the other side of the belt: repeat *1 slip stitch in each stitch of a square, 1 single crochet where two squares join* along the entire length of the belt up to the corner of the last square and hook 1 slip stitch, 1 chain stitch, 1 slip stitch, then 5 slip stitches on the side.

10. Finish with 1 slip stitch in the initial chain stitch of the border. Fasten off and weave in the end.

Scarf

TIME NEEDED: About 6 hours

Looking for a stylish, timeless scarf? Opt for this infinitely versatile one.
And why not add fringes or tassels? Let your imagination run wild!

MATERIALS

4 mm crochet hook
Yarn Used: Elana
(see page 6 for substitution info)
- navy blue (552), 3 balls
- bottle green (611), 2 balls
- baby pink (331), 1 ball

DIMENSIONS

1 square: 6" × 6" (15 × 15 cm)
Scarf: 23.5" × 67.75" (60 ×72 cm)

STITCHES USED

Magic ring (page 10)
Chain stitch (page 11)
Slip stitch (page 11)
Double crochet (page 12)
Triple crochet (page 13)

MAGALIE SQUARE

Squares

For this scarf pattern, make 24 Magalie Squares
(see instructions on page 55) in different colors.

VERSION A

Repeat 12 times
Round 1: baby pink
Round 2: bottle green
Round 3: navy blue

VERSION B

Repeat 6 times
Round 1: baby pink
Round 2: navy blue
Round 3: bottle green

VERSION C

Repeat 6 times
Round 1: bottle green
Round 2: baby pink
Round 3: navy blue

Tip

If you want to make the scarf wider, add an extra row
of 12 squares. If you want to lengthen it, add extra
squares to the ends.

Instructions

JOINING THE SQUARES

When all the squares are crocheted and blocked and their ends are woven in, begin joining using the Elana navy-blue yarn.

Join by single crocheting into the back loops of the squares (see page 18).

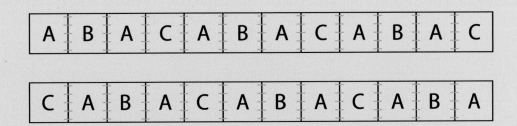

1. Place square A and square B right sides together.

2. Tie off the yarn at the corner of squares A and B with 1 slip stitch: stitch the hook into both squares at the same time, as if it were a single stitch.

3. Crochet 21 slip stitches, always stitching in the back loops of both squares.

4. Following the same procedure, join two strips of 12 squares each, alternating the different versions as shown in the diagram above.

A	B	A	C	A	B	A	C	A	B	A	C
C	A	B	A	C	A	B	A	C	A	B	A

5. Once your strips are complete, place them one on top of the other, right sides together, to sew them together lengthwise. As in steps 2 and 3, attach yarn to the ends of the two overlapping squares and crochet slip stitches along the entire length, working mainly in the back loops of the two squares crocheted together.

THE EDGING

1. Tie the navy-blue yarn to one corner of the scarf with 1 slip stitch, make 1 chain stitch, [2 s.c., 1 c.s., 2 s.c.] in the corners of the square.

2. Work your way around the scarf, repeating *1 s.c. in each square stitch, [2 s.c., 1 c.s., 2 s.c.] in the corners of the squares*.

3. Finish with 1 slip stitch in the edging's first initial single stitch. Fasten off and weave in the end.

Tip
Embellish your scarf with tassels attached to the four corners. See page 88 for instructions on how to make them.

Tote Bag

TIME NEEDED:
About 7 hours

This trendy crocheted bag will spice up any outfit!
Make it in a wide range of colors and patterns, with a variety of squares.
Be inventive and personalize this for yourself or as a one-of-a-kind gift.

——

MATERIALS

5 mm crochet hook
Yarn Used: Tricoton
(see page 6 for substitution info)
- macrame white (101), 2 balls
- camel (118), 1 ball
- Lurex aqua (126), 1 ball
- macrame light gray (103), 1 ball
- macrame yellow (25), 1 ball

DIMENSIONS

1 square: 5" × 5" (13 × 13 cm)
Bag (excluding handles): 20.5" (52 cm) wide × 17" (43 cm) high

STITCHES USED

Magic ring (page 10)
Chain stitch (page 11)
Slip stitch (page 11)
Single crochet (page 11)
Double crochet (page 12)
Puff stitch with three half double crochets (page 14)

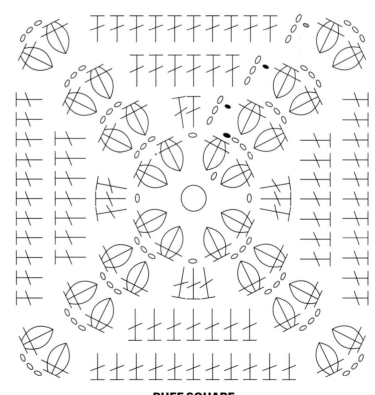

PUFF SQUARE

The Squares

Make 24 Puff Squares (see instructions on page 47),
alternating yarn colors.

VERSION A

Repeat 6 times
Round 1: camel
Round 2: light gray
Round 3: yellow
Round 4: white

VERSION B

Repeat 6 times
Round 1: yellow
Round 2: camel
Round 3: light gray
Round 4: white

VERSION C

Repeat 3 times
Round 1: camel
Round 2: white
Round 3: light gray
Round 4: white

VERSION D

Repeat 6 times
Round 1: light gray
Round 2: Lurex aqua
Round 3: camel
Round 4: white

VERSION E

Repeat 3 times
Round 1: camel
Round 2: yellow
Round 3: Lurex aqua
Round 4: white

Tip

Make the bag larger or smaller by adding or removing a round of squares.

Instructions

JOINING THE SQUARES

When all the squares are crocheted and blocked and their ends are woven in, begin joining using the white yarn.

The structure of the bag is built by joining the squares in pairs, then the strips of squares by crocheting slip stitches in the back loops (see page 18).

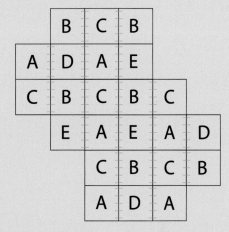

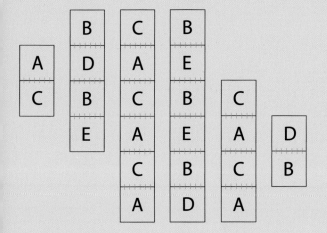

1. Lay out six strips of squares in front of you, alternating the different versions as shown in the diagram above.

2. To sew the squares together, place the first two right sides together.

3. Tie off the yarn at the corner of the squares with 1 slip stitch: stitch the hook into both squares at the same time, as if it were a single stitch.

4. Crochet 14 slip stitches, always stitching into the back loops of both squares, with the last stitch in the next corner.

5. Proceed in the same way to join the six strips of squares.

6. Once you've finished your strips, place the first two on top of each other, right sides together, to sew them together lengthwise. As in steps 3 and 4, attach yarn to the ends of the two overlapping squares and crochet slip stitches along the entire length, working mainly in the back loops of the two squares crocheted together.

7. Repeat until all six strips are joined.

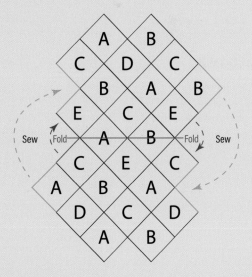

8. Fold the squares together, right sides together, as shown on the previous page. Sew the edges of the indicated squares together, using the same slip stitch technique for the back loops.

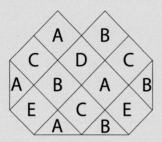

9. Your bag will have the shape shown above.

EDGING AND HANDLES

The edging of the bag and the handles are made on two sides of squares A and B, both on the front and back of the bag.

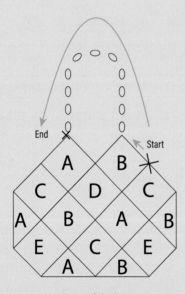

Front of the bag

1. On the front of the bag, with the right side facing you, attach the white yarn in the corner of square B, as shown in the diagram, with 1 single stitch, then do 1 single stitch in each stitch until you reach the next corner of the square and 1 single stitch in this corner.

2. To form the first handle, crochet a chain of 50 chain stitches. Then, coming back to the part already created, crochet 1 slip stitch at the tip of square A.

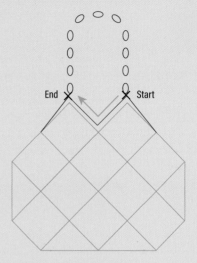

Back of the bag

3. Place the back of the bag in front of you to continue crocheting on the back side. Make 1 slip stitch in each stitch of squares A and B to create the handle, and 1 slip stitch in the starting stitch of the handle.

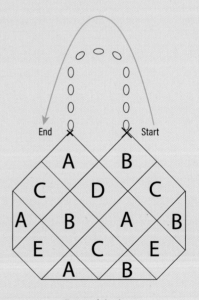

Front of the bag

4. With the front of the bag facing you, crochet 50 slip stitches in the handle chain. Finish with 1 single crochet in the corner of square A.

5. With the back of the bag facing you, crochet the stitches separating the two handles one last time, as in step 3.

6. Continue by crocheting a single crochet in each stitch of square B until you reach the starting point of step 1; do 1 slip stitch.

7. Repeat steps 1 to 6 on the other side of the bag to make the second handle.

8. Fasten off and weave in the end.

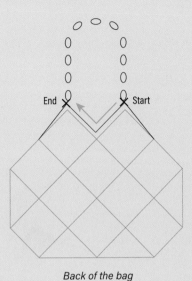

Back of the bag

Tip
Instead of crocheting the handles, another option is to sew on wooden or bamboo handles.

Afghan

TIME NEEDED:
About 8 hours

Looking for a touch of bohemian chic in your home?
This afghan is both quick and easy to make. Use your creativity and
play with colors to create a cheerful feel, or opt for a
solid color for a more elegant look.

MATERIALS

8 mm crochet hook
Yarn Used: Naya
(see page 6 for substitution info)
- cream (6 balls)
- green (3 balls)
- mustard (2 balls)
- taupe (2 balls)
- 1 yarn needle

DIMENSIONS

1 square: 11" × 11" (28 × 28 cm)
Afghan: 35.5" × 49" (90 × 124 cm)

STITCHES USED

Magic ring (page 10)
Chain stitch (page 11)
Slip stitch (page 11)
Single crochet (page 11)
Half double crochet (page 12)
Double crochet (page 12)
Triple crochet (page 13)

BOHO SQUARE

Squares

Crochet 12 Boho Squares
(see instructions on page 61) to make this afghan,
alternating different colors of yarn.

VERSION A

Repeat 3 times
Round 1: taupe
Round 2: green
Round 3: mustard
Round 4: cream
Round 5: green
Round 6: mustard
Round 7: cream

VERSION B

Repeat 3 times
Round 1: mustard
Round 2: cream
Round 3: taupe
Round 4: green
Round 5: cream
Round 6: taupe
Round 7: green

VERSION C

Repeat 6 times
Round 1: green
Round 2: mustard
Round 3: cream
Round 4: taupe
Round 5: mustard
Round 6: cream
Round 7: cream

Tip

Make a larger afghan by using a thicker yarn, or make
a smaller afghan by using a finer yarn.

Instructions

JOINING THE SQUARES

When all the squares are crocheted and blocked and their ends are woven in, begin joining using the cream Naya yarn.

Join the squares by crocheting slip stitches into the back loops of the squares (see page 18).

1. Place square A and square B right sides together.

2. Attach the yarn to the chain stitches at the angle of squares A and B with 1 slip stitches: hook into the slip stitches of both squares at the same time, as if they were a single stitch.

3. Crochet 18 chain stitches, always stitching into the rear strands of both squares.

A	B	C
B	A	B
C	B	A
B	C	B

4. Follow the same procedure to join three strips of four squares each, alternating the different versions as shown in the diagram above.

A	B	C
B	A	B
C	B	A
B	C	B

5. Once you've finished your strips, place the first two on top of each other, right sides together, and sew them together lengthwise. As in steps 2 and 3, attach the yarn to the ends of the two overlapping squares and crochet cast-on stitches along the entire length, working mainly in the back loops of the two squares crocheted together.

6. Sew the last strip to the others in the same way.

THE EDGING

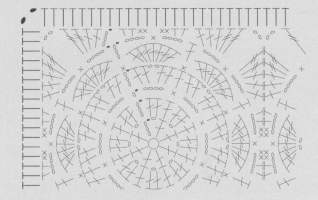

1. On the right side of the project, attach the cream yarn to one corner of the afghan with 1 s.s., make 1 c.s. and 2 hdc. in the same space.

2. Repeat *1 hdc. in each stitch of a square up to the junction of two squares, then make 2 hdc. in the first loop, 1 hdc. in the s.s., 2 hdc. in the second loop* up to the first corner of the afghan. Hook in 2 hdc., 2 c.s. 2 hdc.

3. Repeat step 2 on the other three sides of the afghan.

4. In the last corner, finish off with 2 hdc., 2 c.s. and 1 s.s. in the opening stitch.

5. Fasten off and weave in the end.

Tip

To give the afghan a different look, modify the edging by replacing the half double crochets with another stitch, such as a bobble stitch to create a lacy edge (see page 14).

TASSELS

The tassels add a pretty finish to the afghan and give it extra character.

1. For one tassel, cut 22 11" lengths of cream yarn.

2. Place the first piece of yarn in front of you and place 20 more pieces across its center, perpendicular to the first strand.

3. Tie the single yarn length around the other 20, pulling them tight.

4. Lay the last piece of yarn horizontally in front of you. Place the pile of knotted yarn at its center, so that the knot made in the previous step is above it, and the strands are below it.

5. Tie the horizontal yarn around the others, pulling tight to gather all the strands.

6. Using a needle, separate the yarn strands to add volume.

7. Repeat the same process to make three more tassels.

8. Using the yarn at the top of each tassel, sew them to the four corners of the afghan with a yarn needle.

Tip

Add a big round bead in the center of the tassel to make it look more rounded.

For a more elegant afghan, you can make all the squares in cream.

Pillow Cover

Bring some bohemian spirit into your home!
Here's a crochet must-make: the pillow cover. Use the colors of your choice to match the afghan (page 85) if you like.
You can also adapt it to any size you want.

MATERIALS

8 mm crochet hook
Yarn Used: Naya
(see page 6 for substitution info)
- cream (4 balls)
- taupe (1 ball)
- green (1 ball)
- mustard (1 ball)
- 2 wooden buttons (1"
   diameter)
- 1 yarn needle

DIMENSIONS

1 square: 16" × 16"
(40 × 40 cm)
Pillow cover: 16" × 16"
(40 × 40 cm)

STITCHES USED

Magic ring (page 10)
Chain stitch (page 11)
Slip stitch (page 11)
Double crochet (page 12)
Puff stitch with five half
double crochets (page 14)
Five-stitch bobble stitch
(page 14)

SUNFLOWER SQUARE

Squares

Make a single Sunflower Square (see instructions on page 51) for this pillow, using the colors suggested here, or with any colors you like.

Round 1: taupe   Round 3: mustard
Round 2: green   Round 4: cream

When making the square, you'll notice that on the first three rounds its structure warps. However, the effect will begin to lessen on the fourth round and, after blocking, it will be completely flat.

Instructions

EXTENDING A SQUARE

Once the Sunflower Square is crocheted and blocked and the ends are woven in, move on to the extension process by adding the following three rounds with the cream yarn.

■ Edge extension

Round 1

Attach the yarn to one of the corners of the Sunflower Square, with 1 s.s., 3 c.s., 1 dc. in the same corner.

Repeat 3 times *1 dc. in the next 15 stitches, [2 dc., 2 c.s., 2 dc.] in a corner*.

Crochet another 1 dc. in the next 15 stitches, then 2 dc. in the starting corner, 2 c.s., 1 s.s. in the 3rd initial c.s. of the round.

Round 2

Make 1 s.s. just before the last stitch of the previous round. In this corner, crochet 3 c.s. and 1 dc.

Repeat 3 times *1 dc. in the next 19 stitches, [2 dc., 2 c.s., 2 s.s.] in a corner*.

Crochet again 1 dc. in the next 19 stitches, 2 dc. in the starting corner, 2 c.s., 1 s.s. in the 3rd initial c.s. of the round.

Round 3

Make 1 s.s. just before the last stitch of the previous round. In this corner, do 3 c.s. and 1 dc.

Repeat 3 times *1 dc. in the next 23 stitches, [2 dc., 2 c.s., 2 dc.] in a corner*.

Then crochet 1 dc. in the next 23 stitches, 2 dc. in the starting corner, 2 c.s., 1 s.s. in the 3rd initial c.s. of the round.

Fasten off and weave in the end.

Block to obtain a flat square measuring 16" × 16" (40 × 40 cm).

COVER FLAPS

Once you've made the square larger, you're ready to add flaps at two ends to complete the cover. Flap A will be 8.5" (22 cm), and flap B will be 9.5" (24 cm).

They can be hooked back and forth with cream yarn.

Flap A

Tie the yarn to one corner of the square with 1 slip stitch.

Edge extension

Rows 1 to 9: make 3 c.s. (which count as the 1st dc.), 1 dc. in the next 19 stitches, 1 c.s. and turn.

Finish with 1 s.s. and weave in the end.

Flap B

Attach yarn to one of the two free corners of the square.

Rows 1 to 10: make 3 c.s. (which count as the 1st dc.), 1 dc. in the next 19 stitches, 1 c.s., then turn the piece over.

Finish with 1 s.s. and weave in the ends.

> ## Tip
> Instead of using the button closure, you can instead lengthen the flaps by crocheting 12 rows for part A and 14 rows for part B. This will make both flaps long enough to keep the pillow in place inside the cover.

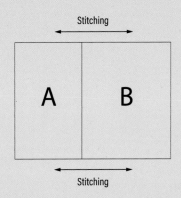

Stitching

A B

Stitching

2. Using a yarn needle, sew a seam on the outer edges to join the different sections. See page 18 for sewing instructions.

3. Attach the buttons to part B: count 10 dc. from the top of the cover and sew on the first button, then count 10 dc. from the bottom of the cover and sew on the second button.

FLAP SEAMS

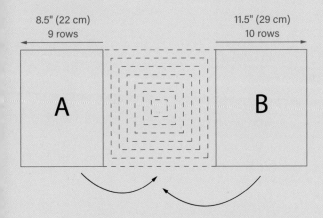

8.5" (22 cm)
9 rows

11.5" (29 cm)
10 rows

A

B

1. Turn over to work on the reverse side. Fold over part B, then part A as shown in the diagram above.

THE TASSELS

See page 88 for instructions on how to make four tassels and, using a yarn needle, sew them to the four corners of the pillow cover.

Acknowledgments

I would like to thank Éditions Eyrolles for giving me this wonderful opportunity to pursue my passion: crocheting!

Thank you to my husband, Victor, for supporting me and encouraging me to pursue my projects fully.

I'd also like to thank Élodie, from Lou Passion, for her trust and belief in my work. Her brand's beautiful yarns are the perfect match for the projects in this book!

Finally, thanks to all of you who have discovered or rediscovered me through this book; I value the amazing discussions you have with me around our shared passion.

About the Author

Hyllam Lefèvre designs crochet patterns for her company Le Crochet de Plume, where she also teaches technique and offers crochet tutorials and inspiration. She collaborates with yarn brands to promote crochet, has been featured in craft magazines in her native France (including *Crochet Pratique* and *Idées à Faire*), and is a stylist for the yarn manufacturer Bergère de France.

www.lecrochetdeplume.com | #lecrochetdeplume